ACROSTIC
ANIMAL ADVENTURES

Animal Rhymes

Edited By Briony Kearney

First published in Great Britain in 2020 by:

YoungWriters®
Est. 1991

Young Writers
Remus House
Coltsfoot Drive
Peterborough
PE2 9BF
Telephone: 01733 890066
Website: www.youngwriters.co.uk

All Rights Reserved
Book Design by Ashley Janson
© Copyright Contributors 2020
Softback ISBN 978-1-83928-911-8

Printed and bound in the UK by BookPrintingUK
Website: www.bookprintinguk.com
YB0441F

Dear Reader,

Welcome to a fun-filled book of acrostic poems!

Here at Young Writers, we are delighted to introduce our new poetry competition for KS1 pupils, *My First Acrostic: Animal Adventures*. Acrostic poems are an enjoyable way to introduce pupils to the world of poetry and allow the young writer to open their imagination to a range of topics of their choice. The colourful and engaging entry forms allowed even the youngest (or most reluctant) of pupils to create a poem using the acrostic technique and with that, encouraged them to include other literary techniques such as similes and description. Here at Young Writers we are passionate about introducing the love and art of creative writing to the next generation and we love being a part of their journey.

From the jungle to the ocean, pets to mythical monsters, these pupils take you on a journey through the animal kingdom and showcase their budding creativity along the way. So we invite you to dive into these pages and take a glimpse into these blossoming young writers' minds. We hope you will relish these roarsome poems as much as we have.

Contents

Bankier Primary School, Banknock

Ruby Duncan (7)	1
Mhairi Pettigrew (8)	2
Allyson Baxter (7)	3
Cody Baxter (7)	4
Jacob M (6)	5
Lewis Dowine (6)	6
Liam Forteath (7)	7

Barling Magna Primary Academy, Barling Magna

Jesse Leckie-Viner (7)	8
Owen Hughes (6)	9
Rosie Hull (7)	10
Isla-Rose Harmsworth-Blyth (7)	11
Lola Hewett (6)	12
Ivy Dobson (5)	13
Evie Marshall (6)	14
Tommy Allum (7)	15
Jake Paul Sellen (5)	16
Ashton Harmsworth-Blyth (6)	17
Chloe King (6)	18
Harley Dilworth (6)	19
Harley Allen (5)	20
James Shayler-Adams (6)	21
Louie Ferreira (5)	22
Harley Palmer (7)	23
Dexter Riley (6)	24
Charlotte Cole (5)	25
Josephine (7)	26
Freddie Adams (5)	27
Marley Adams (6)	28

Moorland Private School, Clitheroe

Olivia Townson (6)	29

Orchard Primary School, Pershore

Freya Green (7)	30
Amelia-May Morris (6)	31
Leonie Summers (6)	32
Ava Phelps (6)	33
Ella Nightingale (7)	34

Prestwich Preparatory School, Prestwich

Fatima Nawaz (7)	35
Zahraa Ali (6)	36

St Ann's CE Primary School, Rainhill

Amy Pullen (7)	37
Alexander Hoogendyk (6)	38
Jack Elliott (6)	39
Lily Sutherberry (6)	40
Poppy Lucas (6)	41
Sophie Lutas (6)	42
Lyla Watts (5)	43
Toby Williams (6)	44
Isla Wynne (5)	45
Maisie Bebbington (5)	46
Fletcher Young (5)	47
Elsa Dalytse (5)	48
Anya C (6)	49
Lucas Garcia (6)	50
Skyla Kermode (5)	51

Hunter McLoughlin (5)	52
Zach Harding (5)	53
Scarlett Thompson (5)	54
Olivia Scott (6)	55
Jack Mills (5)	56
Isabella Hayes (5)	57
Olivia Croxton (6)	58
William Munro (5)	59
Matthew Pickles (5)	60
Vinnie Cuddy (5)	61
William Chean (5)	62
Anastasia Lockett (5)	63
Perla McEvely (5)	64
Joseph Joyce (5)	65
Nancie Cuddy (5)	66
Thomas Rush (5)	67
Fearne Moran (5)	68

St Martin's CE (VA) Primary School, Fangfoss

Maisie Richardson (6)	69
Lois Barnes (5)	70
James Randle (6)	71
Luna Thiel (5)	72
Jessica Stickney (6)	73

St Thomas' Primary School, Wishaw

Niall McGuinness (7)	74
Olivia Burt (7)	75
Kai Kennedy (7)	76
Aidan Higgins (7)	77
Louise Leitch (7)	78
Jennifer Walsh (7)	79
Amelia Ross (7)	80
Samuel Rosulu (7)	81
Victory Nwachukwu (7)	82
Cole Thomson (7)	83
Kyle Miller (7) & Logan	84
Darcy Rooney (7)	85
Amber Rose Cooper (6)	86

Temple Ewell CE Primary School, Temple Ewell

Eliza Goldswain (6)	87
Emily Aylett (6)	88
George Chivers (7)	89
Isabelle Herbert (6)	90
Ethan Dolbear (6)	91
Finley Castle (6)	92
Caison Smith (6)	93
Harriet	94
Damiano Del Duca (7)	95
Harrison Ring (7)	96
Ruben Mora (6)	97
Noah Sharp (6)	98
Leo Fox (6)	99
Harriet Seely (5)	100

Westminster Cathedral Choir School, Westminster

Felipe Samonigg von Staszewski (5)	101
Alastair Black (6)	102
Christopher Valeriano (5)	103
Gabriel Collier (5)	104
Sebastian Gargiulo (5)	105
Orlando Szymanowski Mazzocchi (6)	106
Pietro Pugnali (5)	107
Tom Wilson (5)	108
Alexander Katsambas (6)	109

Woodlands CE Primary School, Woodlands

Harry Tidswell (6)	110
Sam William Amos (5)	111
Charlie Hodgson (6)	112
Dolly Cahill (7)	113
Kieran Maun (6)	114
Phoebe Smith (5)	115
Kealan Jimmy Horan (6)	116
Seb O'Donovan (5)	117
Jasmine Millard-Haigh (6)	118

Zavvi Malik (6)	119
Kimberley Winner (6)	120

Ysgol Gymraeg Ystalyfera Bro Dur, Ystalyfera

Ebony Elkins (6)	121
Joseph John Goddard (6)	122
Owen Davies (6)	123
Lexi Evans (6)	124
Ioan Jones (6)	125
Hari Green (7)	126

The Poems

My First Acrostic: Animal Adventures - Animal Rhymes

Hedgehog

H ow big are they?
E very hedgehog is special
D on't feed them bad food
G ood hedgehogs eat
E ven if they are sore they are special
H ow do they?
O n Christmas, it is snowy
G o and help them.

Ruby Duncan (7)
Bankier Primary School, Banknock

Puppies!

P uppies are so fluffy!
U p on its head there are floppy ears
P retty and so cute
P uppies are all different textures
Y ou don't need to be scared, they are kind.

Mhairi Pettigrew (8)
Bankier Primary School, Banknock

Puppy

P uppies are very cute
U se litter bags for puppy litter
P uppies need a home to live
P uppy love is adorable
Y um yum, pups love food.

Allyson Baxter (7)
Bankier Primary School, Banknock

Marley Dog

M arley
A fter
R ound
L ion
E xcited
Y es

D og
O MG
G od.

Cody Baxter (7)
Bankier Primary School, Banknock

Cat

C an jump high
A cat is friendly
T errible at staying in the house.

Jacob M (6)
Bankier Primary School, Banknock

Dog

D ogs are cute
O range
G ood.

Lewis Dowine (6)
Bankier Primary School, Banknock

Dog

D oor
O ne
G ood.

Liam Forteath (7)
Bankier Primary School, Banknock

Dinosaurs, Dinosaurs

D iplodocus is a large herbivore
I guanadon was a plant-eater too
N othronychus had a beak and huge claws
O viraptor looked like a bird
S pinosaurus had a large sail on its back
A nkylosaurus had an armoured body
U tahraptor was smart, fast and dangerous
R aptors are speedy runners
S tegosaurus had spiked plates on its back.

Jesse Leckie-Viner (7)
Barling Magna Primary Academy, Barling Magna

Gorillas Are Kings

G ripping and hanging on the trees
O *oo-ooo, ooo-ooo, ooo*
R ainforests are his playground
I nsects for their lunch
L arge and big
L ittle gorillas snuggle in
A dventure for the gorilla
S afety in their home.

Owen Hughes (6)
Barling Magna Primary Academy, Barling Magna

Unicorn

U nicorns are soft
N ever scared in the dark
I n the day time, the unicorns hide
C an you always be there?
O ne unicorn is in the forest
R ainbows are above the sky
N ever fear, unicorns are here.

Rosie Hull (7)
Barling Magna Primary Academy, Barling Magna

Unicorn Poem

U nicorns are magic
N ight-time, they glow
I magination is key
C arrots are their favourite food
O lder people don't believe
R eal or not, nobody knows
N ot many unicorns are here anymore.

Isla-Rose Harmsworth-Blyth (7)
Barling Magna Primary Academy, Barling Magna

Amazing Flamingos

F lappy feathered flamingo
L ovely flamingo
A mazing flamingo
M agical flamingo
I nteresting flamingo
N ice flamingo
G entle flamingo
O utstanding flamingos.

Lola Hewett (6)
Barling Magna Primary Academy, Barling Magna

Unicorn

U nicorns are rainbow-coloured
N one of them can fly
I love unicorns
C olours are in their hair
O h, what are they doing?
R iding them would be fun
N othing is better.

Ivy Dobson (5)
Barling Magna Primary Academy, Barling Magna

Unicorn

U nicorns are magical
N ever sad at all
I always love them
C an you always be shiny, unicorn?
O n the path, can you be there?
R eally fabulous
N ever away from here.

Evie Marshall (6)
Barling Magna Primary Academy, Barling Magna

Cheetah

C heetahs are the fastest land mammals in the world
H ave very sharp claws
E at meat
E ndangered
T hey live in Africa and Iran
A re very strong
H unt during the day.

Tommy Allum (7)
Barling Magna Primary Academy, Barling Magna

Giraffe

G igantic
I s patchy all over
R eaches high for the leaves
A frica is its home
F licking tail
F antastically tall
E legant and not small.

Jake Paul Sellen (5)
Barling Magna Primary Academy, Barling Magna

Giraffe Poem

G iraffes live in Africa
I n the zoo you can see giraffes
A t lunch they eat leaves
N ext time I go, I will see the giraffes
T aller and taller they grow.

Ashton Harmsworth-Blyth (6)
Barling Magna Primary Academy, Barling Magna

Elephant

E ars
L ong trunk
E ats from trunk
P eople look after them
H eavy
A ll one colour
N ot meat-eaters
T all.

Chloe King (6)
Barling Magna Primary Academy, Barling Magna

Monkey

M ischievous monkey
O n the trees they live
N aughty monkey
K nows how to climb
E at bananas
Y ucky smells.

Harley Dilworth (6)
Barling Magna Primary Academy, Barling Magna

Fish

F ish live in water
I n a pond is where you will find me
S wimming is what I like to do
H iding is what I do when I am scared.

Harley Allen (5)
Barling Magna Primary Academy, Barling Magna

Giraffe

G ood
I ntelligent
R un
A ppear
F ast
F at
E at.

James Shayler-Adams (6)
Barling Magna Primary Academy, Barling Magna

Tommy

T iny fur ball
O n his wheel
M y pet
M unching his
Y ummy food.

Louie Ferreira (5)
Barling Magna Primary Academy, Barling Magna

A Crab

C rabs in the sea
R un sideways
A round the sea below
B lowing bubbles.

Harley Palmer (7)
Barling Magna Primary Academy, Barling Magna

Crab

C rawling sideways
R unning fast
A lways swimming
B ig and strong.

Dexter Riley (6)
Barling Magna Primary Academy, Barling Magna

Bear

B rown and soft
E ating honey
A ngry growling
R eally sharp claws.

Charlotte Cole (5)
Barling Magna Primary Academy, Barling Magna

Horse

H ooves
O n a ride
R eins
S tirrups
E questrian.

Josephine (7)
Barling Magna Primary Academy, Barling Magna

Cat

C limbing trees
A lways hungry
T errorises birds.

Freddie Adams (5)
Barling Magna Primary Academy, Barling Magna

Cat

C ute and shy
A lways climbing
T ail moving.

Marley Adams (6)
Barling Magna Primary Academy, Barling Magna

Whale/Crab

W ish with their tail
H ave food to eat
A nd play together
L ive underwater
E ach in a line.

C rawling
R unning
A bout
B rave.

Olivia Townson (6)
Moorland Private School, Clitheroe

Guinea Pigs

G ingey is my pet guinea pig
U nder the hay he sleeps all day
I n and out of the run he plays
N ose goes *sniff sniff sniff*
E very time I come to the cage
A ny vegetables he will eat

P urring is the sound he makes
I like playing with my guinea pig
G iving my guinea pig treats is fun
S nuggly cute and fluffy is my pet guinea pig.

Freya Green (7)
Orchard Primary School, Pershore

I Would Love To Be A Unicorn

U nique and magical, a creature of dreams
N ever to date have they been seen
I n the open, the blessing goes wild
C olourful and bright are their swishing tails
O ne-of-a-kind are their beautiful manes
R acing through the fields of magical dust
N ow wouldn't we all love to be a unicorn?

Amelia-May Morris (6)
Orchard Primary School, Pershore

Penguins

P enguins are playful
E ggs are what they lay
N ot nest builders
G oes swimming in the sea
U sually found in the south pole
I t's icy where they live
N o land-based predators.

Leonie Summers (6)
Orchard Primary School, Pershore

Black And White Team

Z ooms across the plains
E ating all the dried-up grass
B asking in the African sun
R unning away from the hungry lions
A nd trying to find a water hole
S leeping foals lay on the ground.

Ava Phelps (6)
Orchard Primary School, Pershore

Magical Me

U nicorn of mine
N early as big as me
I n my bed as
C osy as can be, with
O ne horn
R ight on the top of your head
N early as magical as me.

Ella Nightingale (7)
Orchard Primary School, Pershore

Kitten

K ittens are cute
I t is tiny as well
T hey are very fluffy
T heir favourite food is milk
E veryone likes kittens in my family
N aughty cats I don't like.

Fatima Nawaz (7)
Prestwich Preparatory School, Prestwich

Kitten

K ittens are beautiful
I t likes to run
T igers fight kittens
T he kitten is scared
E very day, the tiger fights the kitten
N o one is scared of the kitten.

Zahraa Ali (6)
Prestwich Preparatory School, Prestwich

The Fastest Animal On Land

C heetahs are the fastest animal on the land
H aving spots to make them camouflaged
E very day, the cheetahs hunt for food
E verything they hunt for is their favourite snack
T he cheetah growls and spits like a cat
A frica is their home, for hunting and playing
H aving their sharp teeth, they can bite other animals.

Amy Pullen (7)
St Ann's CE Primary School, Rainhill

Polar Bear

P olar bears are soft and furry
O n the ice they like to play
L ike to swim in icy waters
A nd they make snow dens
R oll in the snow

B abies are called cubs
E very day they eat seals
A rctic is their home
R eally fast, they can run.

Alexander Hoogendyk (6)
St Ann's CE Primary School, Rainhill

Monkey Business

M onkeys love swinging from tree to tree
O nwards and upwards, they like to be
N aughty little monkeys, playing around
K eeping banana skins to throw on the ground
E veryone, be careful when walking by
Y ou can easily slip on your bum and cry!

Jack Elliott (6)
St Ann's CE Primary School, Rainhill

Sparkles The Unicorn

U nicorns are magical
N ever be afraid
I n your dreams, you will see them
C apturing the hearts of those who believe
O n their horns they sparkle
R ainbows are their friends
N ice unicorns will never end.

Lily Sutherberry (6)
St Ann's CE Primary School, Rainhill

Unicorn

U nicorns are magical
N ever will you see one
I n fairytales, unicorns live
C olours of pink and white and blue
O n my head I have a horn
R ainbows, flowers and stars
N ight Sparkle is my name.

Poppy Lucas (6)
St Ann's CE Primary School, Rainhill

Hippo

H ippos, I love you
I wish I could lie in the mud and the sun, like you
P addling in the river even though you can't swim
P ods are the name of your gang
O pen your big mouth wide to show your big teeth.

Sophie Lutas (6)
St Ann's CE Primary School, Rainhill

Elephantastic

E lephants are fun
L ive in the jungle
E lephants drink with a trunk
P laying in water
H ave big ears
A re grey
N apping in the sun
T usks by their mouths.

Lyla Watts (5)
St Ann's CE Primary School, Rainhill

My Pet

G uinea pigs are cute
U nder the hay
I n the grass
N ibbling carrots
E ating
A pples

P eeing on your knee
I n the hutch
G oing to sleep.

Toby Williams (6)
St Ann's CE Primary School, Rainhill

The Creeping Cheetah

C reeping through the jungle
H oping to catch some prey
E xtremely fast and sneaky
E xtra sharp
T eeth like razors
A nd camouflage spotty fur
H iding in the leaves.

Isla Wynne (5)
St Ann's CE Primary School, Rainhill

Unicorn

U nicorns are beautiful
N ice, quiet and shy
I t has magic in its horn
C arrying happiness to all
O ut in the wild
R unning happy and free
N ow I believe.

Maisie Bebbington (5)
St Ann's CE Primary School, Rainhill

Mr Monkey

M ove through the trees
O pposable thumbs
N aughty monkeys throw nuts
K ing Louie from the Jungle Book
E at bananas
Y oung monkeys ride on their mother's back.

Fletcher Young (5)
St Ann's CE Primary School, Rainhill

Unicorn

U nicorns are special
N ice and sparkly horn
I nteresting and magical
C olourful and bright
O ver the rainbow
R iding in the sky
N ice flowing hair.

Elsa Dalytse (5)
St Ann's CE Primary School, Rainhill

Unicorn

U nicorns are pretty
N ever naughty
I think they can fly
C ute and colourful
O nly a mythical creature
R eally unique
N o one has seen one.

Anya C (6)
St Ann's CE Primary School, Rainhill

Monkey

M ischievous is the animal
O *oh-ooh, ah-ah,* all day long
N ever stops playing
K eeps on swinging
E ating bananas
Y es! It's monkey!

Lucas Garcia (6)
St Ann's CE Primary School, Rainhill

Unicorn

U nicorns are real
N eed lots of love
I n many colours
C an fly
O ften have glitter on them
R un fast
N ever dull, always sparkly.

Skyla Kermode (5)
St Ann's CE Primary School, Rainhill

The Unicorn

U nusual creatures
N ice and happy
I love them
C razy colours
O range, pink, red and blue
R unning in the forests
N ever sad.

Hunter McLoughlin (5)
St Ann's CE Primary School, Rainhill

Zebra

Z ig-zagging through the trees
E lephants are our friends
B lack stripes running down his bottom
R unning away from lions
A lways being brave.

Zach Harding (5)
St Ann's CE Primary School, Rainhill

Panda

P andas like eating bamboo
A sia is where they live
N ot endangered anymore
D id you know, the numbers are increasing?
A dorable and cute.

Scarlett Thompson (5)
St Ann's CE Primary School, Rainhill

The Tall Giraffe

G iant legs
I t eats leaves
R eally tall
A lot of spots
F ound in the zoo
F riendly animal
E yes are pretty.

Olivia Scott (6)
St Ann's CE Primary School, Rainhill

Rabbit

R abbits are so fluffy
A nd they are cute
B ouncing around
B urrowing underground
I nside a hutch
T hey eat lots of hay.

Jack Mills (5)
St Ann's CE Primary School, Rainhill

The Snail

S lowly all around the garden
N ever grows legs
A lways going slow
I s found on the ground
L eaves a slimy trail.

Isabella Hayes (5)
St Ann's CE Primary School, Rainhill

Shark

S harp teeth, sharp fin
H ard, big body
A ttacks for dinner
R ides the waves of the ocean
K nockout speed.

Olivia Croxton (6)
St Ann's CE Primary School, Rainhill

Shark

S wimming in the sea
H unting for prey
A ttacking others
R azor-sharp teeth
K illing machine.

William Munro (5)
St Ann's CE Primary School, Rainhill

Rhinos!

R hinos are heavy
H unted for horns
I n Africa and Asia
N o meat they eat
O dd-toed mammals.

Matthew Pickles (5)
St Ann's CE Primary School, Rainhill

My First Acrostic: Animal Adventures - Animal Rhymes

Lion

L ead me through the jungle
I own the jungle
O ut of the way, animals
N ow hear me roar.

Vinnie Cuddy (5)
St Ann's CE Primary School, Rainhill

Zebras

Z ebras standing
E ating grass
B lack and white
R eally fast
A mazing animal.

William Chean (5)
St Ann's CE Primary School, Rainhill

The Lion Thing

L arge
I n the savannah
O ften seen in zoos
N oisy roar.

Anastasia Lockett (5)
St Ann's CE Primary School, Rainhill

Bear

B rown and big
E xtremely scary
A ngry
R oars loudly.

Perla McEvely (5)
St Ann's CE Primary School, Rainhill

Pigs Are Cute

P igs love mud
I ntelligent animals
G oes, *oink oink*.

Joseph Joyce (5)
St Ann's CE Primary School, Rainhill

Dog

D ogs are family pets
O utside they play
G reat to be around.

Nancie Cuddy (5)
St Ann's CE Primary School, Rainhill

My First Acrostic: Animal Adventures - Animal Rhymes

The Dog And The Postman

D ogs have tails
O ff they run
G rowling at the postman.

Thomas Rush (5)
St Ann's CE Primary School, Rainhill

My Dog

D omestic friend
O bedient and loyal
G reat fun.

Fearne Moran (5)
St Ann's CE Primary School, Rainhill

Cheeky Squirrels!

S quirrels are cheeky
Q uick and speedy
U nbelievably naughty
I ncredible at climbing and hiding
R ummaging in the ground
R un and leap without a sound
E nergetic all the time
L ots of lovely squirrels playing in the park.

Maisie Richardson (6)
St Martin's CE (VA) Primary School, Fangfoss

Unicorn Acrostic

U nicorns are great
N ibbling carrots or lettuce
I t is great for unicorns
C an you find a unicorn?
O h, they are lovely
R unning fast
N *eigh!*

Lois Barnes (5)
St Martin's CE (VA) Primary School, Fangfoss

My Pet Dog

L oves his family
A lways happy
B lack fur
R unning and chasing rabbits
A lways nice
D rinks lots of water
O ld and big
R eally cute.

James Randle (6)
St Martin's CE (VA) Primary School, Fangfoss

The Sparkly Unicorns Poem

U nbelievably
N aughty
I ncredible
C ourageous
O livia
R ainbowy
N aughty
S parkly.

Luna Thiel (5)
St Martin's CE (VA) Primary School, Fangfoss

The Fast Dog

D ogs are sometimes cheeky
O ften they are sometimes soft
G o and fetch, the person says.

Jessica Stickney (6)
St Martin's CE (VA) Primary School, Fangfoss

Titanoboa

T itanoboa is an extinct species of snake
I t lived in extremely hot areas of South America
T his was the largest snake ever discovered
A ll together, twenty-eight individual fossils were found in Columbia
N ew York, Grand Central Terminal had a full-scale model on display in 2012
O n average, titanoboa weighed 2,500lbs
B oidae is a family of snakes where the titanoboa comes from
O rdinary boas are just a fraction of the size of titanoboa
A ll titanoboas became extinct around sixty million years ago.

Niall McGuinness (7)
St Thomas' Primary School, Wishaw

Sausage Dog

S ausage dogs are very long
A wesome sausage dogs can run fast
U sually a puppy eats half a cup of kibble each day
S ausage dogs are very cute
A lways sausage dogs listen
G reat sausage dogs are my favourite type of dog
E very day they go for a walk

D achshund is their real name
O ften they are used to help hunt badgers
G irl dachshunds' babies are in their tummy.

Olivia Burt (7)
St Thomas' Primary School, Wishaw

Crocodile

C rocodiles hunt for fish
R iding on a crocodile is dangerous
O n a river, crocodiles swim very deep
C rocodiles hunt for fish and meat
O n a crocodile, they have sharp teeth and sharp nails
D eep in the river, crocodiles are camouflaged
I n a speeding crocodile, it could be poisonous
L iving like a crocodile, you can live forty years
E lephants can get eaten by a crocodile.

Kai Kennedy (7)
St Thomas' Primary School, Wishaw

Spinosaurus

S mart fish-eater
P articularly, it can swim
I t was tall
N ormally it eats fish
O ccasionally it eats other dinosaurs
S ometimes in the ocean
A ctually, it died in the mass extinction
U ntil the extinction, it was smart
R eally it was big
U ntil it needs to beware near to a megalodon
S cientists have found nineteen bones.

Aidan Higgins (7)
St Thomas' Primary School, Wishaw

Pussycat

P ussycat jumped from the window
U nder the table and pulled the tablecloth
S ay *meow, meow* and spin around
S ix cats belonged to one mummy cat
Y ou love pussycats so I will have a cat
C ome on cat, we need to go to the cat show
A cat and another cat play outside
T raining a pussycat is very hard.

Louise Leitch (7)
St Thomas' Primary School, Wishaw

Elephant

E lephants are bigger than you think
L ittle elephants eat grass with their trunks
E ach elephant weighs 5000kg
P robably been here for about 40,000 years
H as a very loud noise, made with its trunk
A n elephant loves eating grass
N early sixty years it lives for
T akes a drink through their trunks.

Jennifer Walsh (7)
St Thomas' Primary School, Wishaw

Elephant

E ars flapping across the African plain
L ittle elephants have small ears
E lephants have very long trunks
P laying around in the hot sun
H ot sun can make their skin dry up
A ny mud that is around them, they go into it
N othing is bigger than an elephant
T hey have very long tusks.

Amelia Ross (7)
St Thomas' Primary School, Wishaw

Python

P ythons can eat a full grown man in around sixty-four seconds
Y ou can find pythons in the jungle
T he python can grow 20 feet long
H ow it attacks is by wrapping itself around your body
O n summer, pythons hunt for food for wintertime
N ow in these days, pythons are almost extinct.

Samuel Rosulu (7)
St Thomas' Primary School, Wishaw

Cheetahs

C heetahs can run super fast
H unts animals and prey
E ars are small but he still hears very well
E ven faster than a lion
T he world record fastest animal
A woman leaves the family at the age of marriage
H as to live in a cave with its family.

Victory Nwachukwu (7)
St Thomas' Primary School, Wishaw

Spiders

S piders can make webs
P ut poison in their food
I nside the spider is the nylon for its web
D angerous spider is a black widow
E at when the food is webbed
R un quickly with their eight legs
S piders sleep in the middle of the web.

Cole Thomson (7)
St Thomas' Primary School, Wishaw

Monkeys

M onkeys swing from trees
O n the zoo where monkeys bounce
N aughty, fighting each other
K eep leaping around
E at bananas and leaves
Y ou are cheeky monkeys
S catch their heads and armpits.

Kyle Miller (7) & Logan
St Thomas' Primary School, Wishaw

Snakes

S nakes slither all the time
N ever eat people
A lot of snakes camouflage in the grass
K ing of the snakes
E veryone thinks they are cool
S harp teeth.

Darcy Rooney (7)
St Thomas' Primary School, Wishaw

Zebra

Z ebras like eating leaves
E ven they're cute
B lack is their favourite colour
R ushed to sleep in their bed
A lot of zebras play together.

Amber Rose Cooper (6)
St Thomas' Primary School, Wishaw

The Cheeky Cheetah

C runching the grass while it runs in the light green grass
H iding and waiting because it is so hungry
E ating its prey and crunching its bones
E ating it all and trying to catch some more yummy prey
T rying to run faster and faster
A nd when it runs really fast, you will never see it
H umans try to catch them but they are dangerous.

Eliza Goldswain (6)
Temple Ewell CE Primary School, Temple Ewell

Chameleon In The Jungle

C hameleons can camouflage
H ave crystals under their skin
A mazing reptiles
M ainly live in Madagascar
E yes that can swivel in different directions
L ong tongue catches insects
E ndangered species
O nly live two to three years
N obody can see chameleons who are camouflaged.

Emily Aylett (6)
Temple Ewell CE Primary School, Temple Ewell

Panther, Panther In The Jungle

P anthers have really sharp teeth
A panther sneaks up on its prey
N earby there is a bit of meat for the panther, hidden in the tree
T ravelling so far for their big prey
H unting through the large jungle
E very panther has really sharp claws
R acing through the noisy, dense jungle.

George Chivers (7)
Temple Ewell CE Primary School, Temple Ewell

The Silly Cheetah

C heetahs can run very fast
H aving sharp claws helps them grip
E at a bit of nice juicy meat
E njoys eating other animals
T hey chase a long way to get their prey
A cheetah runs across the grassy plains
H ungry for meat, hungry for dinner.

Isabelle Herbert (6)
Temple Ewell CE Primary School, Temple Ewell

Humans Are Amazing

H umans are sometimes very, very hungry
U gly humans all around the world, some nasty, some not
M en and girls all around the world
A mazing humans all over the world, some superheroes, some not
N ight is when we sleep, day is when we don't sleep.

Ethan Dolbear (6)
Temple Ewell CE Primary School, Temple Ewell

The Jaguar Who Owns The Night

J aguars pouncing on their prey
A ll jaguars sneak up slowly on their prey
G rowling as loudly as an engine
U nder a green tree, looking for their prey
A jaguar comes in different types
R unning as fast as a car through the jungle.

Finley Castle (6)
Temple Ewell CE Primary School, Temple Ewell

Happy Hippos

H ippos have big teeth
I n water, they swim fast
P laying and splashing, having fun in water
P addling in squidgy mud
O h no! Hippos are fighting
S wimming and splashing, keeping cool in the hot sun.

Caison Smith (6)
Temple Ewell CE Primary School, Temple Ewell

Mischievous Monkeys

M onkeys swinging high up in the tall green trees
O n the ground, walking around
N aughty monkeys
K eep chattering
E ating yellow bananas all the time
Y elling loudly through the jungle.

Harriet
Temple Ewell CE Primary School, Temple Ewell

The Scary Hyena

H yens are very fast and very hungry
Y esterday, the hyena was hunting for a zebra
E ating a great, juicy zebra
N aughty hyenas hunt for their prey
A t night, hyenas hunt for more delicious prey.

Damiano Del Duca (7)
Temple Ewell CE Primary School, Temple Ewell

The Mean Tiger

T he black, white and orange dangerous tiger
I n the dark, dark, scary cave
G oing out hunting for its delicious prey
E ating its juicy meat
R eady to pounce lots of times.

Harrison Ring (7)
Temple Ewell CE Primary School, Temple Ewell

Terrible Tigers

T he black, stripy tiger is leaping to get its prey
I t is roaring as loud as a car
G rowling louder and louder
E ating as quietly as a mouse
R unning really fast.

Ruben Mora (6)
Temple Ewell CE Primary School, Temple Ewell

Seal

S wimming seals in the sea, swirling, twirling happily
E ating juicy penguins deliciously
A lways swimming up and down
L eaping somersaults round and round.

Noah Sharp (6)
Temple Ewell CE Primary School, Temple Ewell

The Big Bad Shark

S harks eat fish
H ungry sharks looking for tasty food
A cross the swirling waves
R acing for their prey
K illing their prey with one chomp!

Leo Fox (6)
Temple Ewell CE Primary School, Temple Ewell

The Terrible Tiger

T igers are scary
I n the leafy green jungle
G rowling in the dark night
E ating some juicy meat
R azor-sharp teeth.

Harriet Seely (5)
Temple Ewell CE Primary School, Temple Ewell

Tall Giraffe

T he giraffe's neck is long
A giraffe's legs are thin
L ong is its tail
L ofty is its view

G iraffes like to eat leaves
I n the zoo, the giraffes have the best view
R unning giraffes are hard to catch
A lthough they hardly run
F irst, they are my favourite
F urther, they are impressive
E very giraffe has a smile.

Felipe Samonigg von Staszewski (5)
Westminster Cathedral Choir School, Westminster

White Tiger

W hite teeth that are sharp and bright
H ow they give people a fright
I n India, it is rare
T o see a white tiger stare
E lephants can be a safe place to sit

T o watch a tiger do its bit
I dream of the biggest cats, wearing
G iant, wonky hats
E lectrifying claws, terrifying paws, going
R oar, roar, roar!

Alastair Black (6)
Westminster Cathedral Choir School, Westminster

Tarantulas

T errible
A rachnids
R eally dangerous
A rthropod
N ever squished
T oo scary to touch
U gly
L arge as a dinner plate
A re brown.

Christopher Valeriano (5)
Westminster Cathedral Choir School, Westminster

Gorilla

G iant grey ape
O f the rainforest
R ed eyes
I ncredible, amazing animal
L oudly beating his chest
L ooking for his family
A nd protecting his home.

Gabriel Collier (5)
Westminster Cathedral Choir School, Westminster

Deadly Dinosaur

D angerous
I ncredible
N oisy
O versized
S cary
A ggressive
U nstoppable
R oaring.

Sebastian Gargiulo (5)
Westminster Cathedral Choir School, Westminster

Happy Gorilla

G reen trees
O *oh-ooh*
R oar
I n the forest
L azy
L eaves and sticks
A frica.

Orlando Szymanowski Mazzocchi (6)
Westminster Cathedral Choir School, Westminster

Crab

C an swim into the water,
R ather than other
A nimals can live on land as well. Take a big
B reath, this is my poem!

Pietro Pugnali (5)
Westminster Cathedral Choir School, Westminster

Shark

S ly creature in the sea
H unting tiny fish
A ngry at humans
R ed blood in the water
K illing stingrays.

Tom Wilson (5)
Westminster Cathedral Choir School, Westminster

Dog

D ogs are cute
O urs is cuddly
G entle and fun.

Alexander Katsambas (6)
Westminster Cathedral Choir School, Westminster

Billy The Sheepdog

B illy is a sheepdog who lives on a farm
A round the fields he runs
R ounding up the sheep, keeping them from harm
K eeping the sheep together is his job
I f Billy is good, he gets a treat from farmer Bob
N ight-time comes and Billy goes to bed
G etting lots of rest before the day ahead.

Harry Tidswell (6)
Woodlands CE Primary School, Woodlands

Unicorn

U nder the trees sit lots of tigers
N ext to the trees are cheeky monkeys and spiders
I n the rainforest there are lots of snakes
C raftily sneaking up on people eating cakes
O utside the forest is an extremely huge snake
R oaming the swamp for chocolate cake
N obody goes to the forest.

Sam William Amos (5)
Woodlands CE Primary School, Woodlands

Dinosaur

D inosaurs were colossal
I magine finding a fossil
N ow they are extinct
O ther than birds, there's no other link
S tegosaurus was about the size of a bus
A nd its brain was the size of a walnut
U nder water they lived too
R ounding up schools of fish to eat.

Charlie Hodgson (6)
Woodlands CE Primary School, Woodlands

Squirrel

S neaking nuts wherever they go
Q uickly bolting up the trees
U nbelievably cute
I ncredibly clever
R ed squirrels are becoming rare
R apidly running through the woods
E mpty nut shells scattered on the floor
L eaping from branch to branch.

Dolly Cahill (7)
Woodlands CE Primary School, Woodlands

Ferocious Dinosaur

D inosaurs lived 230 million years ago
I nteresting fossils from long ago
N o one knows how many there were
O ne was called T-rex
S o fast and mean
A stegosaurus had horns
U nfriendly giant beasts
R oar!

Kieran Maun (6)
Woodlands CE Primary School, Woodlands

Sparkle The Unicorn

U nicorns are magical
N eighing and galloping
I ncredible at flying
C olourful and glittery
O n its head it has a horn
R ainbows in its hair
N ever lets us see it.

Phoebe Smith (5)
Woodlands CE Primary School, Woodlands

Lion

L ifespan ten to fourteen years in the wild
I n captivity, lions live for more than twenty years
O ften known as the king of the jungle
N early 80% of baby lions die within the first two years.

Kealan Jimmy Horan (6)
Woodlands CE Primary School, Woodlands

The Rapid Raptor

D own in the river
I n the river
N ow, there are fish
O ver by the rocks is a
S hark
A t tea time
U nder the water
R aptor eats the fish.

Seb O'Donovan (5)
Woodlands CE Primary School, Woodlands

Dragon

D eep red, fierce dragon
R aging through the town
A ngry when he is hungry, stomping and
G nawing his way around
O range fire breathing
N aughty little dragon!

Jasmine Millard-Haigh (6)
Woodlands CE Primary School, Woodlands

Terrifying Tiger

T igers are wild
I n the jungle they hide
G ets ready to fight
E very day, they hunt
R oars ferociously!

Zavvi Malik (6)
Woodlands CE Primary School, Woodlands

Panda

P o, his name is Po
A sia
N ature
D o
A nimal.

Kimberley Winner (6)
Woodlands CE Primary School, Woodlands

Mystical

M y unicorn is beautiful
Y ellow, pink and blue
S ome say they don't exist
T he name of my unicorn
I s summer because she is bright and warm
C ome and see my unicorn
A nd play with me, we can
L isten to my poem and it will make you happy.

Ebony Elkins (6)
Ysgol Gymraeg Ystalyfera Bro Dur, Ystalyfera

Giraffe

G iraffes are tall
I tower over all animals
R un at 60kmh
A frica is my home
F ruit is my favourite
F ood to eat
E lephants are my friends.

Joseph John Goddard (6)
Ysgol Gymraeg Ystalyfera Bro Dur, Ystalyfera

Puppy

P uppies like to hide,
U sually they go outside.
P uppies like to play together,
P laying with their toys.
Y es, I love puppies!

Owen Davies (6)
Ysgol Gymraeg Ystalyfera Bro Dur, Ystalyfera

Cat

C ute and cuddly
A dorable
T abby.

Lexi Evans (6)
Ysgol Gymraeg Ystalyfera Bro Dur, Ystalyfera

Alfie's Adventures In Pet Landia

D oughnuts
O range
G iving.

Ioan Jones (6)
Ysgol Gymraeg Ystalyfera Bro Dur, Ystalyfera

Under The Sea

D ancing
O ysters
G iggle.

Hari Green (7)
Ysgol Gymraeg Ystalyfera Bro Dur, Ystalyfera

Young Writers Information

We hope you have enjoyed reading this book – and that you will continue to in the coming years.

If you're a young writer who enjoys reading and creative writing, or the parent of an enthusiastic poet or story writer, do visit our website **www.youngwriters.co.uk**. Here you will find free competitions, workshops and games, as well as recommended reads, a poetry glossary and our blog. There's lots to keep budding writers motivated to write!

If you would like to order further copies of this book, or any of our other titles, then please give us a call or order via your online account.

Young Writers
Remus House
Coltsfoot Drive
Peterborough
PE2 9BF
(01733) 890066
info@youngwriters.co.uk

Join in the conversation!
Tips, news, giveaways and much more!

YoungWritersUK   @YoungWritersCW